GOD AND YOU

PRAYER AS A
PERSONAL RELATIONSHIP

GOD AND YOU

PRAYER AS A PERSONAL RELATIONSHIP

William A. Barry, S.J.

PAULIST PRESS
New York/Mahwah

Excerpts in chapter 12 of an article by William A. Barry, S.J., are reprinted by permission of *Praying*, Kansas City, Missouri

Library of Congress Cataloging-in-Publication Data

Barry, William A.
    God and you: prayer as a personal relationship / William A. Barry.
        p. cm.
    Bibliography: p.
    ISBN 0-8091-2935-3 (pbk.): $4.95 (est.)
    1. Prayer.   2. Spiritual life—Catholic authors.   I. Title.
BV215.B37 1987   87-24612
248.3'—dc19   CIP

Published by Paulist Press
997 Macarthur Boulevard
Mahwah, New Jersey 07430

Printed and bound in the
United States of America

Contents

To my sisters
Peg, Mary, and Kathleen
with love and gratitude

Preface

This little book about prayer does not derive from theory, but from the experiences of hundreds of people who have brightened my days since I began to give spiritual direction about sixteen years ago. Thus the book is experiential, not theoretical. Because it is experiential, it is limited by my experience even though my personal experience has been enriched by the sharing of experience of many others. Those others are mostly Roman Catholic and the majority have been priests or religious or people in training for ministry. Moreover I am a Jesuit and so my experience is colored by the spiritual tradition inspired by Ignatius of Loyola. I have had very little experience of the tradition of image-less prayer or of prayer inspired by Eastern mysticism. Ignatius was fond of the term *Deus semper maior,* God the ever greater. He would be the first to say that God is also greater than the experience of all those who have been inspired by his genius. This book then must be taken for what it is, one limited human being's effort to offer his experience to those who might be helped by it.

I do want to make one further point about the experiential nature of the book. What I say in this book about prayer and God and what happens to people who consciously try to develop their relationship to God is not based on pious hopes or wishful thinking. I am talking about what has actually happened to people although to protect the identities of persons I have changed details, used fictitious names, and sometimes developed fictitious examples based on real cases. What I say may not be true of all people who are consciously in relationship with God, but it is true of some. I can testify to that. So I do invite the reader to try it. You might like it. In fact, the book is written with the hope that readers may, like the kids who watched Mikey eat the new cereal in the famous TV ad of a few years ago, notice that "Mikey likes it" and try this way of prayer.

A word about the gender of God. I have adhered to the traditional usage of masculine pronouns and adjectives when referring to God. God is, however, neither male nor female since gender differentiation is a human condition. Moreover, God has not been nor is always experienced as masculine. We will refer to the experience of God as feminine in the book. I hope that those who predominantly experience God as feminine will not be offended by my traditional usage or even worse made to doubt the validity of their experience.

Finally I must say thanks to the hundreds of people in the United States, Canada, Ireland, Jamaica, Guyana, Trinidad and Brazil who have trusted me with their most precious gift, their experience of God. I am especially grateful to all who read the chapters at various stages and were so helpful: my father, my three sisters, Peggy, Mary, and Kathleen to whom I have dedicated this book, my late cousin John Shea and his wife Madeline and their children Paul and Mary, Clare and Wally Ritchie and the members of the prayer group in Hamilton, Patricia Y. Geoghegan, Annie Toner, Virginia Sullivan Finn, John Carmody, Mary Spratt, R.C., Gerald Calhoun, S.J., Joseph Fallon, S.J., William Stempsey, N.S.J., James Carr, N.S.J., Michael Fitzgerald, N.S.J., Myles Sheehan, N.S.J., Joseph McCormick, S.J., James Kane, S.J., Thomas Bubnack, N.S.J., Ellen Nelson, R.S.C.J., Mary Guy, O.S.U., and Philomena Sheerin, M.M.M. Without their encouragement and suggestions the book would never have been completed.

Prayer as Conscious Relationship

A number of years ago I saw a photograph entitled "School Prayer." In it one sees first graders in prayer. Their faces are very serious, most have their eyes closed, and most have strained, tense, even squinty looks. Their hands are tightly folded. It is a rather funny picture until you begin to think about what we might be teaching children about prayer and about God. Most of us adults have had the same kind of teaching. When you think of prayer, what comes to mind? Going to church or chapel? Closing your eyes? Getting down on your knees? Thinking deep thoughts? Do you get a little nervous? Do you think about devotions and rosaries or the Book of Common Prayer? I suspect that most of us would figure that prayer is something holy people do a lot while we just occasionally do it. I wonder how many of us think of our Sunday church services as prayer.

While we may have some real qualms about prayer and wonder whether it is for the likes of us, at the same time we are curious. For instance, you have started to read this book. Books on prayer are becoming a hot item in publishing circles. Admittedly, they do not top best seller lists, but they sell well enough that publishers are on the lookout for new ones. No need to go into the reasons for this renewed interest in prayer. Let us take it for granted and take your interest for granted. In this chapter I propose to discuss prayer as a conscious relationship with God and then in future chapters to spell out some of the implications of such an understanding of prayer. My hope is to help people to develop their personal relationship with God, in other words, to help people to pray.

In our creeds we affirm our faith in God as our Creator and Redeemer. We call God our Father, Jesus our Brother, and the Holy Spirit the Giver of life. We affirm that Jesus died for our sins and rose again for our justification. Let us just think for a few minutes about the implications of these creedal statements for prayer. Whether we know it or not, the creed says, God is in relationship with each and every created thing in the universe and in relationship to the whole of it. He continually creates and sustains in being everything and everyone in the universe. In the words of the theologian John Macquarrie God lets-be every being. Hence, God is in relationship to every being whether that being is aware of the relationship or not. The same line of reasoning can be followed out for every other creedal statement about God. The Son of God, the Word made flesh, is brother to all human beings on the face of the earth whether they know it or not. The Holy Spirit is the Giver of life to those who are unconscious of the gift as well as to those who are conscious. So God, Mystery itself, is always and everywhere in relationship to us and to the whole universe, and, because he is God, consciously in relationship.

Does God want us to be consciously in relationship with him? Old and New Testaments and the experience of men and women down through the ages testify that he does. The Bible is a record of how God continually tried and tries to awaken human beings to the full reality of who they are, namely his beloved children. Moreover, he wants us so awake and aware for our own good. Human beings who do not know their real father or mother, for example, suffer a lack that will probably show itself in a sense of rootlessness or of not knowing who they really are. So, too, unawareness of the God who is so intimately in relationship with us may show itself in occasional anxiety about the meaning of life, or in a frantic search for answers to life's mystery, or in overwork or overindulgence of some kind. Knowing who we are—in our depths—is salutary and freeing even if a bit daunting. So God does want us to be in conscious relationship with him. And conscious relationship is prayer, another way of saying that prayer is the raising of the mind and heart to God.

The remarkable thing about God is that he will not force himself on us. He continually tries to arouse our interest in him, to invite us to awareness and a deeper relationship, but he leaves us free to blind ourselves to his presence if we wish, or to refuse to respond even if we are aware of his presence.

First, however, let us say a few words about how God tries to arouse our awareness of him. You are riding in a car with someone else driving and you turn around and are stunned by the beauty of a sunset. You pick up a two-week old baby and feel a sense of awe and wonder as you touch her tiny hand. Your husband has just had a heart attack and is hovering between life and death in the intensive care unit; you start to pray for him, but find yourself blurting out to God, "You don't give a rap for us!" and you sense a presence there in sympathy with you. You and your wife have just made love after a great evening together; as you lie beside her you are filled with a gratitude for all of life that brings tears to your eyes. You see a picture of an emaciated Ethiopian mother and child; your heart seems to stop beating for a second and you wonder what you can do. In these and many other ordinary events of life God may signal his presence and his care.

As noted earlier, we are free to pay attention to these experiences, these possible overtures or communications of God, or not. We can let them drop out of awareness as quickly as we forget a stomach cramp when it goes away. Or we can wonder about the experience and its meaning. For example, I might note how I felt when I saw the sunset and realize that spontaneously I had whispered "Wow!" and meant it as praise of God. I still feel rather exhilarated and have a desire to recover a relationship with God that has been on the back burner in recent years. In other words, such experiences may lead us to realize that we have been missing something in our lives and that we want something more.

What is the something more that we want? There may be a forest full of answers to that question. I may want to pass an exam, to find a new job, to meet a mate. I may want the cure of my sick mother. I may want a sense of purpose in life or the lifting of depression. I may want a family rift healed or the victory of the Democratic party. I may want to know that God cares for me personally. I may want to know Jesus and what he stood for better. I may want to become more like Jesus in my attitudes and values. Scratch any of these desires a little, even the seemingly most self-centered and materialistic, and we will find that we want to know something about God and his relationship to us.

If I seriously ask God to help me find a better job, for instance, what do I mean? At the surface, I suppose, I am asking God to make something good happen for me. If I think about the request a bit more, I may realize that what I most want is to know that he cares for me and has a loving providence in my regard. In other words, all our desires of God, even for material things, reduce to a desire for a sense of his relationship to us. We want to know how God is toward us.

Thus far we have established a working definition of prayer as conscious relationship. The relationship is based on God's actions to establish it and his desire that we become conscious of who he is and wants to be for us. Our consciousness depends on our willingness to pay attention to God's actions, or at least to experiences that might be the actions of God, and to let our desires for God be aroused.

Before ending this chapter let me spell out a few implications of the working definition. First, when I become conscious of God's actions, no matter how dimly, then I am praying, even if I do not say a word. If you think of prayer as conscious relationship, any time of the day or night can be prayer time. I can be walking along with someone, both of us admiring the fall foliage, and it is a conscious relationship even if no words are spoken, as long as I am aware of the other's presence. So too with God. Second, we can make prayers of petition more understandable. Why ask God for something if he is all-knowing and loving? He does not need information, e.g., that my best friend is sick and I want him to get well. But if prayer is relationship, the issue is not information, but whether I believe he cares how I feel and whether I am willing to let him know what I feel and desire, that is, to reveal myself. Third, distractions in prayer are as normal and ordinary as they are in any relationship. You can be with someone you deeply love and be in a deep conversation and suddenly wonder if you put out the lights in the car. So too in prayer. Also distractions during a conversation with a friend sometimes come because you do not want to hear what the friend is saying or because you are bored with the friend. The same thing can happen during prayer. Finally, if prayer is just conscious relationship, it is not something esoteric, for saints and mystics. It is open to anyone, including the likes of us.

2

Getting To Know God

When my mother was dying of cancer, she said that she prayed every night that God would take her in her sleep. I asked her what God was like, and she answered, "He's a lot better than he's made out to be." She was referring, of course, to many of the things said about God from pulpits and in talks. Her own experience had taught her differently about God. How did she learn about God? Not from books because my mother read very little. It was simply from praying a lot. And the prayers she said were mostly the rosary and devotions, prayer forms not much in favor these days. One time I asked her what happened when she prayed. During her response she said something like this: "Sometimes while you're saying your prayers, you go deep and you know he's listening to you and you to him." Apparently my mother had gotten to know the living God and found him a good deal more benign than he had been made out to be.

· We have defined prayer as conscious relationship and noted that many people seem to want to enter into such prayer. That is, they want to know God better. How do we go about getting to know him better? We can begin by asking how one gets to know anyone. You can get to know something about another person by asking someone else about him or her. Often enough when we are first interested in someone, that is how we go about it. If the other

16

is famous or an historical figure, we can read about him or her in a book. Without being too conspicuous, we can sometimes watch a person from a distance to see how he or she is acting with others. People have used all these ways to get to know God. Note that I asked my mother what God was like for her. People have also learned about God from reading the Bible or books on theology or on the spiritual life. Many have learned about God by reading Augustine's *Confessions,* Teresa of Avila's *Autobiography,* Julian of Norwich's *Showings,* the Little Flower's *Autobiography,* Thomas Merton's *Seven Storey Mountain* and many other such confessional books. Such reading is like watching from a distance to see how God behaves with others.

One thing is clear. To get to know someone better, we have to spend a bit of time at it. But if we want a more personal relationship rather than a vicarious one with another, we have to take the chance of a personal encounter. In the case of God even making the efforts just described can open the door to a personal encounter. He seems ready to take any opportunity for closeness. Have you ever been attracted to someone and just hoped that he or she might be interested in you? Many people, past and present, have found God to be like that, ready to take the slightest bit of interest in him as a chance to enter a closer relationship. Yet the question remains: Is there anything we can do to develop a closer relationship with God?

We already have one clue. Time spent in trying to get to know the other is necessary. We do not develop (or keep) any close relationship without spending some quality time together. My mother spent time in prayer daily, and thus, it seems, gave God a chance to let her know what he was like. I believe that it does not really matter what one does during such times as long as one desires to spend the time with God, just as it does not matter what one does with a new friend. You can go walking, have dinner, see a movie together, or attend a lecture, and you are getting to know one another. So too with God. You can read the Bible, say a rosary, recite prayers from a book, walk in the woods, listen to music, visit the aquarium, sit in an armchair with a beer, watch television, or take a bath. As long as you are aware of wanting God to be present, you are in conscious relationship and therefore praying. But notice that you do take the time.

Another thing about time. You can spend a little or a lot of time with a friend depending on the circumstances. We forget that quality time can be a quick phone call in the middle of a busy day just as much as hours together in deep conversation. If we put off talking with a friend until we are able to arrange the latter, we might not get to it for weeks, and we might miss the opportunities suggested by a thought of the other in the middle of the day. Often enough, people think that "real" prayer requires a lot of time. If we see prayer as conscious relationship, then we can begin to school ourselves to respond to those moments when the mind and heart turn to God. Of course, it is a good idea to set aside longer periods for the relationship with God just as we would do with a good friend.

It is to these longer periods that I now turn. How do we spend time with God? As I have indicated, there are many ways of doing so, from devotions to reading to walking in the woods. I would like to discuss a few possibilities suggested by the notion that relationships deepen and develop when the people involved pay attention to one another. We presume that God is paying attention to us. The question is: How do we pay attention to the invisible, mysterious Other we call God? Given the concerns and anxieties each one of us has, we find it hard, often, to pay attention to a flesh-and-blood human being whom we love. How much more difficult then with God whom we cannot see or hear or touch, it seems. How do we let God reveal himself?

Again, my mother affords a clue. She did something she liked to do and this gave God a chance to bring her "deep." She liked to say the rosary and to say her novenas.

Many people find that strenuous efforts to control their distractions in order to pay attention to the quiet voice within do not help them. Such efforts often lead to the self-absorption that shows itself in questions like "How am I doing?" or "Am I doing it right?" Such efforts also lead to discouragement. But people do benefit from spending time doing something they like which is in the broad sense contemplative—e.g., listening to music, watching the stars, looking at and smelling flowers, walking in the woods, luxuriating in a warm bath, remembering favorite people. They do something, in other words, that will attract their attention away from their self-concerns and anxieties. Again, my mother provides an example. Whenever she drove in a car, she was nervous and, of course, more nervous the worse the weather. She would always take out her rosary and pray it while at the same time taking part in whatever conversation might be going on. Once she said that all her nervousness disappeared when she was praying the rosary in the car during a snowstorm. She felt in God's hands.

We can look at the same process in another way. We do something we like to do and ask God to be with us. It would be like telling a new friend that I would like him or her to enjoy what I enjoy or to know what I enjoy. When I do this, I can ask my friend how he or she likes what I like. So too, I can invite God to make his presence felt as I do what I like to do.

People are surprised at what happens when they approach prayer in this way. At first, it may not even seem like prayer, especially for those of us who have a narrow view of what can be religious. But with encouragement they try it and gradually find such times enjoyable and relaxing. They may find themselves feeling joyful or grateful and sense that someone is present who loves and cares for them. They may find themselves spontaneously talking interiorly to God, pouring out feelings of gratitude, or relief, or whatever. Somehow or other they, too, have found that he is a lot better than he's made out to be.

What we have been discussing is a kind of prayer that can be called contemplative. This word evokes images of mystics in rapture or even levitating. But I am using it quite simply to mean a prayer of relationship, of conscious presence to one another. The English theologian Martin Thornton uses the term empathetic prayer and quotes the Oxford Dictionary's definition of empathy: "the power of projecting one's personality into (and so fully comprehending) the object of contemplation."

Traditionally nature and scripture have been the privileged places suggested to Christians for such contemplation. These are not the only ones, as I have suggested. One can look at paintings, listen to music or luxuriate in a bath and hope that the Lord will make his presence felt. But traditionally Christians have contemplated God's creation in hopes of meeting him, and they have contemplated scripture. Let us look at how one might do such a contemplation of creation. In the next chapter we shall discuss the contemplation of scripture.

Contemplating God's creation means looking, listening, smelling, tasting, touching first of all; it does not mean brooding about creation or pondering theological theories about it. We can spin grand theories about how God reveals himself in trees and flowers, stars and sea, but few of us take the time to look at, smell, taste or touch one of these creatures long enough to let God reveal himself as the maker of the creature and indwelling in it (or him or her). So the first thing that recommends itself is to take time to sense the flower, the wind, the stars, the tree, etc. Just doing this can be a way of relating to God. Think of how an artist feels when she sees you admiring her sculpture; there is a communion between the two of you as you touch and admire it. Your interest in and response to the work of art is a communication to the artist even if you say nothing out loud. So too with the contemplation of God's creation. You can be praying just by consciously sensing what he has made. Of course, you may want to say something "out loud," as it were. You may "ooh" at a beautiful sunset and realize that you are praising the Creator. In effect, many psalms and poems are just such "oohs and aahs" but touched by the poetic genius. God, I'm sure, is pleased by such psalms and poems, but also by our less poetic, more mundane words or grunts or smiles.

While contemplating creation in this way, even more

intimacy is possible if we want it. A couple of times we have said that we can ask God to make his presence known, to reveal himself while we are contemplating. This kind of language sounds mystical, a far cry from what seems possible to the likes of us. I mean something rather ordinary in the main, but we should not lose sight of the fact that many people have very intense experiences of God. People do, for example, hear an inner voice that seems to be that of God. Still most of the time God's communication is more ordinary. For example, a man was walking along a beach at night and saw the moonlight touch with silver the crest of a wave. He was delighted and felt at peace and in the presence of someone who himself delights in such things. He felt that God was close and loved him even though he often drank too much and got angry with his family. He knew that God knew all about him and yet loved him, and he felt freer than he had in years.

Recently I was walking near the seashore. It was a bright, crisp autumn day; the sun shone through golden and red leaves and sparkled on the blue water. All of a sudden I felt a tremendous sense of well-being, a great gratitude and a strong desire welling up in me. On reflection I knew that I had felt the touch of God and a strong desire for him. One sixty-three year old man described an experience he had as a child while outside on a summer day: "In the heart of the child that I was there suddenly seemed to well up a deep and overwhelming sense of gratitude, a sense of unending peace and security which seemed to be part of the beauty of the morning ... " (quoted in Edward Robinson, *The Original Vision: A Study of the Religious Experience of Childhood*). The contemplation of creation can be a door for meeting the Creator himself.

3

Contemplating Scripture

In the last chapter we discussed ways of getting to know God and ended by describing a way of contemplating creation that gives God a chance to reveal himself. We noted that the other privileged place suggested to Christians for contemplation is scripture and now we look at what the contemplation of scripture might entail.

Just as creation is not God, but his creature and a privileged place to meet God, so too with scripture. How do we use scripture in order to meet the living God? The simplest answer, and one that has the longest tradition, is just to read it. Through the centuries Jews and Christians have experienced the living God speaking to them in their circumstances through the bible. Theologians ponder what it means to say that the bible is the word of God, but the reason why they ponder the question at all is because so many people in synagogue and church have experienced the word precisely as word of God. So the first advice to those who want to get to know God better is: read the bible and let its words speak to you.

The bible is a very complex entity, as we all know. God has used many voices and many literary genres to convey to his people who he is and wants to be. In order to read the bible with profit one does not have to be a scripture scholar or a theologian. God's word is there for all his people whether they are learned or not. Still it can help one's contemplation to know something about how a particular book of the bible was put together and for what purpose. So someone seriously interested in the use of the bible for prayer would do well to have in the house some kind of introduction to the books of the bible. Liturgical Press of Collegeville, Minnesota has a series on the Old Testament and one on the New Testament that make available the results of scholarly studies in readable form. *The Jerome Biblical Commentary* is also a good one-volume source.

In broad strokes I would like to suggest some ways of contemplating scripture that give God a chance to reveal himself. I begin with the assumption that most of scripture is written as imaginative literature. Even the historical books of the Old and New Testaments are imaginative literature much more than they are historical records as we might understand history. The books of the bible are written so that the people of God might know in their hearts and imaginations as well as in their minds who God is and how he wants to relate to them. In a real sense they aim to make God present now. For them to achieve their purpose, therefore, we must let them catch us up into their world in much the same way that we let a good novel or play or poem grasp us.

Take, for example, Psalm 103 which begins:

Bless the Lord, O my soul;
and all that is within me,
bless his holy name!
Bless the Lord, O my soul,
and forget not all his benefits,
who forgives all your iniquity,
who heals all your diseases,
who redeems your life from the Pit,
who crowns you with steadfast love and mercy,
who satisfies you with good as long as you live,
so that your youth is renewed like the eagle's.

As I read these lines (aloud, if possible), what happens within me? I may feel a welling up of praise, a feeling of great gratitude. The poem, in other words, has reminded me of all that God has done for me and caught me up in its own rhythms. I may also feel nothing and wish that I could feel grateful to God. Perhaps it is not the day for this psalm, or perhaps my reaction will alert me to a need for some healing from God. For example, I do not feel particularly blessed or whole because of a fight with my husband last night. I can tell God how I feel and ask him for some balm and some perspective on the fight. The point is that reading the psalm has opened a door to a conversation with the Lord.

Suppose that I am feeling lost and sinful and out of sorts and yet desire to know that God still loves and forgives me. I can well imagine how the Israelites must have felt when they were in exile in Babylon. Jerusalem and the temple had been razed and they had been herded off as servants and slaves by their conquerors. Their prophets had told them that all this had happened because of their sins. They must have felt abandoned by their God. Yet at this, one of the bleakest moments of their history the Israelites heard the words of Isaiah 43:

> Fear not, for I have redeemed you;
> I have called you by name, you are mine.
> When you pass through the waters I will be with you;
> and through the rivers, they shall not overwhelm you;
> when you walk through fire you shall not be burned,
> and the flame shall not consume you.
> For I am the Lord your God,
> the Holy One of Israel, your Savior.
> . . .
> Because you are precious in my eyes,
> and honored, and I love you,
> I give men in return for you,
> peoples in exchange for your life.
> Fear not, for I am with you.

What I want is to hear these words as spoken to me in my present need. So I ask the Lord to let me know that he loves me and forgives me in the same way, and then I read the text slowly (again aloud, if possible) and just sit quietly. I may, at first, be too agitated and self-concerned even to concentrate on the text. Once again I ask God for help to hear him speaking to me personally and I reread the text. I can say to him whatever comes into my head and heart and come back repeatedly to the words of Isaiah. The magic does not always work. More often than not, however, something happens, and I end up feeling more peaceful or relieved or grateful.

I can also use a gospel story of healing in much the same way. We all remember the story of Bartimaeus, the blind beggar at the end of chapter 10 of Mark's gospel. He hears that Jesus is nearby and he begins to shout, even against opposition, "Jesus, Son of David, have mercy on me!" I can imagine myself crying out to Jesus in the same way, asking him to take pity on me. Then perhaps I too will hear Jesus say: "What do you want me to do for you?" I can tell him what I want and ask him to heal me or hold me or whatever.

The gospels are particularly apt for this kind of imaginative contemplation because they contain so many vivid stories. The best way to get to know Jesus is to ask him to reveal himself and then to read a gospel passage and let it stimulate our imaginations. If we do this over time, we gradually will get to know what Jesus is like, what he values and loves and what he hates. We will also notice whom we identify with in the gospel stories. Sometimes we will feel like Peter, sometimes like John, sometimes like Martha, sometimes like the rich young man or the pharisee. As Jesus becomes more and more a real person of flesh and blood to us, we also become more and more aware of the many ways we relate to him.

Sometimes people get concerned about deluding themselves by letting their imaginations run free with a text of scripture. First of all, we remind ourselves that scripture aims at engaging our imagination as much as our mind. It is imaginative literature, as we noted earlier. Second, we pay attention to the scripture text itself and let it dictate where our imagination will go. Third, we trust the Holy Spirit who dwells in our hearts to guide our imagination, to reveal the truth of God to us. In these post-Freudian days we are aware of the influence of unconscious motives on our behavior and especially aware of their influence on our imagination. As a result we may be even more mistrustful of imagination than Christians of former times. At the same time we need to recall the doctrine of the indwelling Spirit who, as St. Paul says, "helps us in our weakness" and "intercedes for us with sighs too deep for words" (Rom 8:26). One of the "unconscious" influences on our imaginations, we can say with faith, is the Spirit of God. Admittedly, not every moving image is a revelation of God; admittedly, we can delude ourselves. In a later chapter we shall take up in more detail how one can tell the difference between experiences that are of God and those that are not. This is called discernment of spirits in the history of spirituality. For now let us just trust our imaginative reading of scripture and see where it leads. We can reverence it as a privileged place to meet the living God.

Developing Our Relationship with God

We have been talking about prayer as conscious relationship. Relationships are dynamic, not static, as we all know. There are good days and bad days in any close relationship. Indeed, there can be relatively long periods of intensely deepening involvement followed by relatively long periods of emotional distance. Close relationships touch us at deep levels where we can as easily recoil as reach out. In this chapter I want to discuss the process of developing our relationship with the Lord.

How do we develop a relationship? In other words, how do we get to know and love someone? First of all, we have to be interested in or attracted to the other. If we are self-absorbed, we will never get to know another. Nor will we get to know the other personally if we just think about him or her all the time and never interact; this is a fantasy relationship. Moreover, we cannot get to know another if we monopolize the conversation. It is clear that if we want to know another person we must spend time with him or her and ask him or her for some self-revelation. So in the last two chapters we have spent time on contemplation, on ways of letting the Lord reveal himself.

The next question is: What do friends reveal to one another? What do we want to know about someone in whom we are interested? I suppose that we do want some information. We like to know where our friends were born, how many brothers and sisters they have, what schools they went to, and so on. But we are obviously not satisfied with information. We want to know how they felt about their parents, their siblings, their schools. In other words, we want to know their heart: their moods, passions, likes and dislikes, and values. And ultimately we want to know how they feel about us. A relationship without such knowledge of the heart would be like a relationship with a robot. And in fiction and movies even robots are given some affectivity, some heart; otherwise they are very uninteresting.

So too in the relationship with God information alone can be singularly uninteresting. Catechism answers about one nature and three persons, for example, do not attract us much except as an intellectual conundrum. We want to know what God cares about, values, loves and hates. And that is what God reveals in scripture. He tells the Israelites that he loves them, that they are precious in his eyes. He says that he will spit the lukewarm out of his mouth. Jesus weeps over Jerusalem and calls the pharisees whitened sepulchres. He yells at Peter in anger: "Get behind me, Satan!"

Of course, our own interest in the Lord's affectivity is more personal as well. I not only want to know how he felt toward John, but even more how he feels toward me. Do you love me? Do you forgive me? Do you care for me the way you cared for Israel? Do you delight in what I delight in? Tell me about yourself, Jesus, so that I can know you better, love you more, and follow you more closely. These are the desires we have as we approach the Lord.

Relationships also involve mutuality. If I want you to reveal your heart to me, then I must be ready to reveal my own to you. The same is true of my relationship with the Lord. It may be objected that God already knows everything about me and that therefore it would be superfluous, even impertinent, to want to reveal myself to him. As I said in an earlier chapter, it is not a question of giving God information. Rather the issue is one of trust and transparency. Even though I may say that God knows everything about me, I often find myself strangely reluctant to become aware of certain feelings and attitudes and even more reluctant to admit them to God. What happens in any relationship happens even more surely in the relationship with the Lord: the closer we get, the more I learn about the other, but also the more I learn about myself, and some of what I learn is not pretty. So we need to look more carefully at this issue of self-revelation to the Lord.

As we approach any new relationship or a new level of intimacy in an on-going relationship, all of us experience both attractions and repulsions. We are excited and afraid. In the initial euphoria we may not be as aware of the fears, but eventually they crop up. We may be afraid of rejection, of being found wanting, or of the new demands that may be made of us, etc. In the case of God we are probably most deeply afraid of being swallowed up in his immensity, of losing our very selves, as well as of the demands he might make on us. When these "negative" emotions begin to surface, then we will know that it is not so easy to be transparent before the Lord. How can we let him know that he terrifies us, for instance, or that we do not like some of his attitudes in scripture? If we are loath to tell a close friend some of our negative feelings toward him or her, how much more diffident are we with almighty God. No matter how often preachers tell us that God is love, deep down we all harbor some pretty strong feelings about him that go back to childhood and some of the stories we heard about him then. I do not want to belabor the point. We can all recognize the reality of what I am saying.

Revelation of self does not come all at once. For one thing we humans could not take it if God revealed himself all at once to us. There is a profound truth in the fear expressed in the Old Testament that one would die if one saw God face to face. In his Spiritual Exercises Ignatius of Loyola makes a curious, but profound statement about God: "I will ponder with great affection how much God our Lord has done for me, and how much He has given me of what

He possesses, and finally, how much, *as far as He can,* the same Lord desires to give Himself to me according to His divine decrees" (italics mine). One can almost sense a pathos in that statement, that God is limited in his ability to give of himself and feels the limitation. Of course, the limitation lies in the fact that we whom he loves so much are finite. But the limitations may also come from the past experience each of us has had with parents and other authority figures and with teachings about God. We may be very skittish about letting God get close. We may also be angry at God for some of the hurts life has dealt us, even while at the same time being attracted to him; it is hard to let someone get close when we harbor a secret resentment toward that person. So God has to be very patient and infinitely sensitive with us, and he is. Few people are knocked off their horses as St. Paul was.

We, too, will only gradually reveal ourselves to the Lord, and we need patience with ourselves. Still it is good to recognize that what most often hinders the development of a relationship is not so much unwanted or even unsavory feelings directed at the other, but the unwillingness to reveal at least some aspect of the feelings to the other. Just think of what happens when you are angered and made resentful by a close friend and you are afraid to let the friend know. Usually the friendship becomes more and more polite and distant. We may not like some of the feelings and thoughts that arise in us as we relate to God, nor some of his affective responses either. However, relationships deepen as both persons become more and more transparent before the other—in other words, when we are willing to let one another see ourselves as we really are. Relationships stagnate when certain strong affects are consciously or semi-consciously hidden from the other.

An example may help. Once at the beginning of a retreat a man told me that his last three retreats had been pretty boring and that he expected the same this time. Still that was O.K., he said, because at least he got a rest from the rat race. I asked him if he liked it this way. After a good deal of hemming and hawing he admitted that he would prefer a more lively relationship with the Lord. So I suggested he tell God that he had this desire and then do some things he liked to do that might give God a chance to answer. Not much happened for two days, but on the third day he realized that he had been repressing strong feelings of anger at God for an incident in his life. The reason for the repression was that he was also genuinely grateful to God for so many other things. So the only way the anger could come out was in boredom. Once he admitted the anger to the Lord his retreat prayer became much more alive.

One of the biggest stumbling blocks to progress in prayer is the desire to be "good" before the Lord. I could never admit to being depressed or angry or sexy or whatever I consider "bad" in his presence. Another way to describe the same block: I pretend to enter the relationship at a "better" place than I actually am at. For instance, in the case of the man just mentioned, he could not admit to being angry at God at this time. What we fail to realize is that feelings are not really in our control. We cannot will to like or dislike someone. We cannot will anger or love or, for that matter, orgasm. Affects are elicited from us by internal or external stimuli. We may not like some of our affective reactions to the Lord, but in his presence we cannot will them away. Our relationship with him will develop the more we can just admit who we are even if we wish we were different.

An interesting thing happens as we grow in intimacy and thus in transparency. We learn more about ourselves as well as about the other. We become more fine-tuned and sensitive to our own inner states and thus have more and more to "say" to the other. I put the word "say" in quotation marks because often enough as two people become more and more intimate, they communicate as much without words as with them. This is especially true of the relationship with the Lord.

Images of God and Prayer

Relationships develop through mutual transparency. Easy enough to say, much more difficult to practice. First of all, as we have already indicated, human beings are finite and limited and cannot take in the Mystery we call God. At the deepest level of our being we are both attracted to knowing and loving that Mystery and terrified of it. Augustine said: "My heart is restless and it will not rest until it rests in Thee." He might as truthfully have continued: "but it is also afraid to rest in Thee." As I pondered this ambivalence while drafting the chapter, the two contradictory statements of Robert Frost's poem, "Mending Wall," came to mind. "Something there is that doesn't love a wall," and "Good fences make good neighbors." Within each one of us, I believe, there is both a desire not to have a wall between God and oneself and a feeling that such a wall is absolutely necessary if one is to remain oneself. It might be good for us to ponder this ambivalence at more length so that we become more at ease with ourselves, and more patient.

God loves us with an everlasting, creative love. That creative love brings us into being and sustains us. We are God's beloved children, and deep within our beings we know this fact and yearn for full union with God, a union that feels like a reunion. At or near that very same depth, however, we blanch at the awesomeness of such a union.

Some who have tried to describe or explain this instinctive recoil attribute it to a fear of being swallowed up, of losing one's self. Others attribute it to an unwillingness to accept finitude, limitation and death. Whatever the source the resistance to union has strong and deep roots. God with infinite patience tries to convince us to let his love, like the frozen-ground-swell of Frost's poem, break down the wall, to convince us of the paradox that the more closely united we are to God the more ourselves we are. If God can be so patient, then we, too, can try to be patient with ourselves and to continue to ask God to break down our walls.

The ambivalence we have just been describing keeps us from letting God come close, or rather, since God is already close, even closer to ourselves than we are, as Augustine says, keeps us from *experiencing* God's closeness. This ambivalence may well only die when we do, but we can hope that the attraction to union will grow stronger and the resistance weaker the more we get to know God. There are, also, however, hindrances to our willingness to become more and more transparent before God. That is, just as there is a deep ambivalence in us that both wants and fears God's transparency, his revelation of himself to us, so too there are in us blocks to our desire to reveal ourselves to God. These blocks, I believe, derive from our images of God.

A woman once said that she could not read the bible without feeling depressed and guilty. She felt that everywhere she turned in the bible God was condemning people like her for their lack of faith and their sinfulness. It was apparent that something prevented her from seeing that the bible is filled with reassurances of God's merciful, forgiving love. What prevented her from seeing? I did not have a chance to talk to her at great length, but I would venture to say that she had an image of God which made him all-good, all-powerful, all-seeing, and a relentless pursuer of sin in his creatures and an image of herself as of little goodness in God's eyes. With such an image of self in relation to God she could not apply to herself or perhaps even notice such words as these of Isaiah: "Can a woman forget her sucking child, that she should have no compassion on the son of her womb? Even these may forget, yet I will not forget you. Behold, I have graven you on the palms of my hands" (Is 49:15–16).

We shall return to this woman in a moment, but for now let us ponder the way we encounter God or anyone else, for that matter. Whenever we meet a new person, he or she activates in us self-other images (called schemata by some psychologists) that have been built up over the years through interactions with significant people. For example, Mary may remind me of my sister Lucy, and my initial reactions to Mary may be negative or positive depending on my relationship with Lucy. If my relationship with Lucy was very poor, and feelings of resentment and inadequacy infuse that self-other image, then Mary may not get a chance to prove to me that she is a different kind of person than Lucy was. I may feel hostile toward her and read her reactions to me as demeaning and uncalled for and walk away. Or I may feel so inadequate that I come across that way, and Mary quickly loses interest in continuing the conversation. If, on the other hand, my relationship with Lucy had been a mixed one, some good elements, some bad ones, then Mary and I may have a chance to get acquainted, and I will learn through experience what Mary is like in her own right. But it remains true that no relationship, including the relationship with God, develops without being tinged, at least at the beginning, by the residue in our psyches of our past relationships.

Our image of self-in-relation-to-God begins to develop in childhood and is heavily influenced by our relationships with our parents and other older relatives or caretakers. As children we are little, vulnerable and impressionable, and we have only a child's capacity for making sense of a very complex world. Even with the best of parenting we can develop a self-in-relation-to-God image that is very black and white. "If I am good, i.e., kind, sweet, obedient, pure, etc., then God smiles on me; if I am bad, i.e., angry, sullen, sexy, sassy, etc., then God is angry at me." Such an image may not change very much as we

34

grow up because we may not pay much attention to God during our adolescence and early twenties. If in our thirties we begin once again to take religion seriously and try to pray, we may be hindered by the image of God that lingers on from childhood and which still strongly colors our felt relationship with God even though our ideas of God are now more adult and more nuanced.

Let's return to the example of the woman I met. She was intelligent and well educated and knew that God is defined as love, that God so loved the world that he gave his only Son for our salvation. In her mind she could say that God loved her, but as soon as she tried to relate to God in a personal way, she felt judged and condemned. This occurred most forcefully when she tried to use scripture for prayer. It seems that she felt "not good" before a God who looked with baleful eyes at her. In other words, there were realities in her, perhaps anger and resentment at people she "should" love, that her God found unacceptable; hence, she felt, he could not love her. Such feelings depressed her. So she avoided anything that would evoke such feelings, and scripture was a prime source. She would obviously find it very difficult to let God come close and to let him see her as she really is.

Many of us who begin to take a more personal approach to prayer have to reckon with the effect of such residues of childhood images of God on our present relationship with God. Perhaps our image of self-in-relation-to-God is not so starkly black and white as the one we just looked at, but we may well blanch the first time we become aware of an undesirable feeling or image when we are praying. Then we quickly become aware of how fragile is our belief that God forgives all, loves us as we are. We try to banish the feeling or thought or image from consciousness in order to "concentrate on God" or on the text of scripture we were contemplating. But usually that effort does not work. We find that the unwanted feeling or image keeps pushing its way into consciousness. So we may find ourselves straightening pictures on the wall, planning what we will do when prayer is over, thumbing through a book that is lying nearby, or finally just quitting prayer for the day. We may not understand what has happened; indeed, we may not even be aware that "something happened." If we think of the prayer period at all, we may just chalk it up to "one of those days" when prayer is dry. But if something significant for our developing relationship with God has occurred, we may well find that prayer is dry and difficult at least for the next few days. We may notice a reluctance to pray, for example, or a lot of fidgeting and "distractions" when we pray. God may seem very distant, even unapproachable. We may find ourselves reverting to old ways of praying, ways that fill up the time but leave us feeling relatively cold and unmoved. Feelings of discouragement may arise, and we may give up the efforts to develop a more personal relationship with God as a "bad job," something not meant for the "likes of us."

What has happened? More than likely the rise to consciousness of the unwanted or undesirable feeling or image—let's say it is anger at some life hurt, such as losing my mother as a five-year old—has activated an image of God as intolerant of anger, especially anger at him. I recoil with fear, fear that God will reject me for feeling this way. The recoil reaction is most often spontaneous and quickly blocked from consciousness. Rationalizations take over, if they are needed. "The anger is totally irrational. God is all-loving and knows what is best for me." "This anger is a distraction, a temptation that keeps me from prayer." "I must be getting tired from overwork." The clue that I may be resisting an initiative of God to draw me into deeper intimacy with him is that prayer remains distracted and the relationship distant for days afterward. In fact, things may remain so until I go back to the issue of my anger and admit to myself and to God that I am angry because of my mother's untimely death and then see how God actually reacts. When people are able to take such a step, they find out that God is not rejecting, not angry. In fact, he seems closer, warmer, more caring than before. They feel freed of a great load and more grateful than ever to God. Their image of self-in-relation-to-God has begun to change toward a more adult, realistic one.

Such changes often come hard and take a long time and much patience with ourselves. For instance, when I become aware that the anger is getting in the way of a closer relationship with God, I may be too frightened to tell God directly that I am angry at him for the death of my mother. At this point it helps to realize that in any relationship I can only do and say what is possible to me at any one time. I might wish that I were feeling less afraid of God, but if that is the way I am, the issue is: What can I do now? What is possible to me? Perhaps I can tell God that I am afraid of him and ask his help to be less afraid. If I do this, I am being as honest and transparent in the relationship as I can be now. If I persist in this desire, I will gradually find my fears dissipating and the anger slowly surfacing until finally I can tell God how angry I am that my mother died when I was five.

It needs also to be emphasized that one clean breast of the anger may not be the end of the affair, just as one expression of the fear may not be enough to overcome the fear. Our images of self and God sit deep within us and have had a long time to develop. They do not change easily. We could become discouraged that a week after a breakthrough such as described in the last paragraph we find ourselves feeling the same fear, the same anger. Recall that the same thing happens to us in our other relationships. You have been hurt by a friend, for example, and harbor a resentment for days. But the friend asks pardon repeatedly, and you do not want to lose the friendship. Finally in an emotional meeting you forgive the friend and make up. Does it not often happen that the resentment flares up anew periodically after this, so much so that your friend may begin to wonder if the relationship will ever recover? It can be discouraging. We need to recognize that our personalities only change gradually and only if we patiently stay in significant relationships through thick and thin. This is true of our personalities in relationship with God as well.

While we are on the subject of the image(s) of God we have, it might be helpful to recognize that our image of God has feminine as well as masculine characteristics. Theology tells us that God is neither male nor female, but we have experience only of male and female persons. Traditionally God has been addressed and spoken about as male—so traditionally, in fact, that attempts at more inclusive (and more accurate) language in reference to God are often treated as bordering on heresy. My guess is that this issue will only be resolved by a patient listening to people's actual experiences of God in prayer. My experience has been that most people begin their more serious and conscious attention to prayer with a sense of God as masculine. This is what we have been taught since childhood. But God is experienced as Mystery who has both masculine and feminine characteristics. This is understandable given the fact that our image of self-in-relation-to-God develops out of our matrix of self-in-relation-to-father and -mother images. As we develop our relationship with God, experience shows what parts of our images are analogous to the real God, what parts are distortions of the real God. In the course of that development some people find that at least for a time the image of God becomes feminine. It seems the only way that God can convince us that she/he is beyond gender categorization and that masculinity is not the favored gender. Interestingly, women seem less threatened by such a shift in image than men.

My purpose here is not polemic. I began this chapter with the notion that our images of God, which are unavoidable for us human beings, can be sources of resistance to the development of our relationship with God. It has happened that a new development in relationship has been slowed or resisted because the person involved became frightened or anxious at the gender shift God seemed to be making. All our images of God are in some sense idols which ultimately want to imprison God. Perhaps the strongest idol is the image of God as male.

If we stay with the relationship with God, gradually letting him know who we really are and letting him let us know who he really is, we will find ourselves changing and our image of God as well. We will become more tolerant of our weaknesses and limitations as we realize that God is tolerant. But we will also notice ourselves being more able to avoid our worst sinfulness, more forgiving of ourselves and others, more willing to give the benefit of the doubt to others. Gradually we will come to believe the fundamental truth of Christianity, that God loves the world, yes, but that that world includes me with all my warts and moles and more and more other people, even those I really do not at first care for. I find that in my heart I am becoming more Christian, and it is because of my developing relationship with the Lord, not because of strong resolutions. In the process my image of God is becoming more and more approximated to the image of God Jesus seems to have had. These developments are another sign that our prayer is going in the right direction. We are on a life-long journey of getting to know the real God and in the process realizing our best selves.

6

Imagination and Prayer

This is probably as good a place as any to discuss at more length the issue of imagination and fantasy in prayer. In the history of spirituality there have been two main ways of prayer. One way stresses imageless, quiet prayer. In our day this way is perhaps best exemplified by the use of centering prayer. One of the best known teachers of this kind of prayer is Basil Pennington, the Cistercian monk of St. Joseph's Abbey in Spencer, Massachusetts. It is a very helpful way of giving ourselves a chance to get in touch with the Mystery we call God at the center of our being. The other way is exemplified by the Jesuit tradition which advocates using all of our faculties in prayer: sensation, imagination, mind, will. Since this is the tradition with which I am most familiar, this book has stressed the use of sensations and images in prayer. This stress should not be taken to mean that my way is normative for everyone. Both traditions have a venerable history, and I suspect that most people can be helped to meet God by trying both ways. It could be that some kinds of personalities prefer one way to the other, but I am not prepared to try to distinguish personality types and their affinities for prayer forms. I would encourage people to use whatever helps them to meet the living God. Methods are only means to that desired end. When the end is attained, i.e., when God is encountered, then the relationship itself takes over.

But we need to say something about the use of imagination as a method that many have found very helpful to meet God. In an earlier chapter we have already noted how one can use imagination in contemplating scripture, especially the gospels. We let the words of a gospel scene touch our imaginations much the way poetry or a novel might, asking the Lord to reveal himself to us in the process. We can imagine ourselves as actually a part of the scene.

At different times in our lives we will find ourselves identifying more with one character than another. In times when, for example, we feel lost and unsure of our path, we may identify with Bartimaeus, the blind beggar of Mark 10, who cries out, even against opposition, "Jesus, son of David, have mercy on me!" The opposition may be within us, in the inner voice that tries to tell us that prayer is futile. Then we, too, may have to cry out all the more, and we, too, may hear deep within us Jesus saying, "What do you want me to do for you?" And we respond with our need to see, "Master, let me receive my sight, let me see my way." And then we can pour out our heart's pain to him.

At another time we may find ourselves surprised at our reactions to a gospel scene. One man, for example, was reading the section in Mark 3 where it says, "And he went up on the mountain, and called to him those whom he desired; and they came to him. And he appointed twelve, to be with him, and to be sent out to preach and have authority to cast out demons" (Mk 3:13–15). He found himself getting angry, and he did not understand why. He asked the Lord to help him to understand what was happening. Gradually it dawned on him that a Christian does not have much choice of who his companions are going to be. He realized that he was angry at a number of the people with whom his Christian living had brought him together. The resentment had been building up unawares and affecting his happiness and his effectiveness in work. The realization in itself freed him of some of his apathy, and he was also able to ask Jesus to help him to look at his companions as also Jesus' companions.

Another example: People are often surprised at how difficult it is to let Jesus wash their feet as he washed the feet of his disciples at the last supper. When they recoil, they now understand Peter's reaction which before had seemed incomprehensible. As they ponder their reaction and ask the Lord's light on it, they come to sense that their real sin is the unwillingness to accept Jesus' forgiveness and to believe that they are loved and, therefore, lovable.

People obviously differ in their imaginative abilities, or, perhaps better, in the kinds of imagination they have. Some seem able to visualize in colorful detail the whole gospel scene, almost as though their imaginations were creating a technicolor movie. Others have a vivid auditory imagination so that whole conversations seem to go on in their heads and hearts. Others, and here I count myself, do not seem to see or hear much at all, but to feel the story and the characters in a way that is hard to describe. This last group can be envious when they listen to the more vivid descriptions of others and may even feel discouraged at their "lack of imagination." Actually everyone has an imagination. If you wince when someone describes the impact of a hammer hitting his thumb, you have an imagination; if you can enjoy a good story, you have an imagination. Imaginations differ; we need to let God use the one we have and not bemoan the one we do not have.

I would like to suggest some other ways to use our imaginations to help us to develop our conscious relationship with the Lord. It can be a great help for any intimate relationship to recall in memory and imagination its history. Families love to go over old photographs together to recall the good times, laugh and rekindle warm feelings. It binds them together even if such recall also reminds them of painful times as well. All of us can say that the person we have become is largely due to the significant relationships we have had in life. There is a good deal of truth in the statement of a husband, wife, or close friend of long-standing, "You have made me who I am today." Our relationship with the Lord has a history too, but much of it is hidden from our eyes. Only he knows all that history. How can we come to share at least some of it?

Here is one way that has helped many people. You take a quiet moment to recall God's presence and then you ask him to show you how he has been in your life, to show you your personal salvation history, as it were. Then you recall some place or person from childhood, perhaps your family home or one of your parents, and you let the images and thoughts come as freely as possible, that is, without consciously trying to steer them. For instance, if a lot of the memories revolve around your father, do not try to steer them toward your mother, to give her equal time. Just trust that God through his indwelling Spirit will direct the images and memories so that you will come to know how he has been in your life. Whenever you feel like saying something to the Lord, do it just as you would make comments while going over a family album with family members. At another time you can begin with a memory from grammar school days and use the same process. In this way over a few days or weeks you can cover your whole life up to now and perhaps the words of Psalm 139 will take on a new meaning.

> For thou didst form my inward parts,
>> thou didst knit me together in my mother's womb.
> I praise thee, for thou art fearful and wonderful.
>> Wonderful are thy works!
> Thou knowest me right well (Ps 139:13–14).

Another use of the imagination was suggested to a group I was part of. We found it quite helpful. You close your eyes and try to relax by sitting comfortably and breathing deeply, paying attention to your breathing in and breathing out. It also helps to relax to pay attention to the various parts of your body in succession, beginning from your head and descending to your feet. Just notice the sensations in each part. Then imagine yourself looking down a long corridor at the end of which is a closed door. Slowly you walk toward it. As you get closer, you notice that it has a name on it. Finally you see that the name is your own. It's your room, and only you have a key to it. You unlock it and enter, closing the door behind you. What is it like? How would you have set it up? Imagine it any way you would like. Settle down in it and enjoy it. There is a knock at the door. You go over and open the door. It's Jesus asking whether he can come in. Do you want to let him in? If you do invite him in, do you sit down, stand or what? What would you like to say to him or ask him? Stay with him there as long as you wish or can. When it's time to leave, you can tell him you have to go, you can invite him to stay or to go with you, or you can ask him to leave so that you can have a few minutes by yourself. When you are ready to leave, close the door behind you and walk down the corridor and then gradually become aware again of your body and breathing and open your eyes. The beauty of this exercise for those for whom it works and is helpful is that they now have a room in their imagination to which they can invite Jesus whenever they wish.

Finally there are some people with vivid, creative imaginations who have been able to let God use this gift as a way to develop the relationship. One woman I know spent the good part of a retreat on a vacation with Jesus during which time she was able to pour out her heart to him and ask his advice about how to handle some of the troubling issues of her life. Some of her times of prayer were spent imaginatively outdoors, some before a fireplace. Near the end of the retreat Jesus left and headed back to the city, and she knew that this was his way of telling her that he would be with her in her daily life. A man spent a long time in prayer on a camping trip with Jesus. In the course of the trip the basic issue of their relationship emerged, namely the man's ability and willingness to trust Jesus enough to tell him what was really on his mind. Some people create whole stories out of incidents in the gospels. One woman followed Jesus on the way of the cross in vivid detail, even to the point of helping him to his feet when he stumbled and staying close to him when the guards became menacing and tried to drive her away. Nothing could keep her from going with Jesus.

When we use our imaginations in prayer in any of these ways, we are aware that much of what happens is our own product, based on our own past experience. How can we be sure that the whole thing is not just a fanciful daydream that we piously call prayer? My first answer is a trust in tradition. God has, it seems, used the imagination of saints like Ignatius of Loyola, Francis Xavier, and Margaret Mary Alacoque to draw them into a very deep intimate friendship with him. And then I would point to a need for discernment, but a discernment that does not take as a starting point suspicion of our human nature, but trust that God has made us good. It is a profound insight of Ignatius to note in the beginning of his rules for discernment that God's presence to those who are searching for him is signaled by positive emotions: gentleness, peacefulness, quiet confidence. If our use of the imagination leads to such feelings as well as to an increased faith and hope and love and a desire to know God and Jesus more, then we can have confidence that the Lord is using our imaginations for his purposes and our good. Doubts about such prayer can be seen as temptations, especially if the doubts and questions allow of no clear answers, that is, remain only as nagging doubts and questions and do not lead to new and better ways to pray.

The main burden of Sebastian Moore's brilliant book, *Let This Mind Be in You,* is that sin is the denial of one's goodness and desirability, the denial, in other words, of God's creative love which has made us to be lovely and good. Of course, we can fool ourselves, but the best way to make sure that we do fool ourselves is to start by suspecting everything that we feel, imagine, think and want as somehow wrong or at least tending toward the wrong.

In this matter of discernment it also helps to have someone we can talk to about our prayer. I will say more about a spiritual director in a later chapter. For now it suffices to note that it is very helpful for our confidence in the direction of our prayer life to be able to describe what is happening to someone who is interested in listening to it. Just the act of describing to another what happens when we pray helps us to be more attentive to the conscious relationship with God and more appreciative of the gifts we have been given, even if the other person does nothing more than listen attentively and sympathetically. We ourselves often see where we are being led by God and where we are straying from the path. It is even more helpful, of course, if the listener can also by judicious questions and comments help us to see that our prayer is leading toward a deeper intimacy with the Lord that fits the pattern of how God has dealt with people even if each person is a unique exemplar of the pattern.

The main point of this chapter is to encourage people to use whatever helps them to meet the living God. In the tradition imagination has been a great help. If this is your way, trust it as one of God's gifts to help you know him better.

7

Emotions and Prayer

If we want to develop any relationship, we must be willing to reveal and have revealed to us emotions, feelings, values as well as ideas and information. This is usually easy enough when the emotions are warm and positive, although even here it is difficult for many people to accept tender feelings directed toward them. We have already noted that God must work with infinite patience to get us to believe that he really does love us with an everlasting love. I want to emphasize that we need such a primordial experience of God's love for us before we can move on to let him reveal to us our sinfulness or the darker sides of our personalities. It is a great pastoral mistake that so much of the teaching and preaching we are exposed to stresses sinfulness. No doubt we are sinners, but only God can reveal to each one of us our actual sinfulness, and we will only let him do it if in our hearts and bones we know that he really is on our side. Hence, pastoral and spiritual practice must bend every effort to help people to have that primordial experience, the experience to which my mother, I believe, was referring when she said that God is a lot better than he's made out to be. A British psychiatrist, J. S. MacKenzie (in *Nervous Disorders and Character*), put it this way:

The *enjoyment of God* should be the supreme end of spiritual technique; and it is in that enjoyment of God that we feel not only saved in the evangelical sense, but safe; we are conscious of belonging to God, and hence are never alone. . . . It is not our submission God wants but our spontaneous love and fellowship. . . .

I would urge readers to spend time asking God to help them to have such a foundational experience. It is the experience of knowing that one is lovely and loved that precedes any real sense of having marred that loveliness. It is the experience of knowing deep in one's heart that one is the apple of God's eye. It is the experience of hearing what Jesus heard: "You are my well-beloved." It is not enough to tell ourselves that God loves us; we need to feel that love that desired us into being, that saw everything, including me, as good, indeed very good (Gen 1). So spend time with the creation story of Genesis 1, asking the Lord to help you to believe and experience, to experience and to believe all the more, that you are God's beloved. Spend time with the beginning of Isaiah 43, that passage we referred to in Chapter 3. Time spent in such prayer is time exceedingly well spent and leads to the foundational experience upon which all Christian, indeed all religious living is based.

Even with such a foundational experience it is still difficult to let God see us with certain feelings and attitudes. We are reluctant to have anyone we love see us jealous or enraged or unforgiving. I believe that people find it most difficult to reveal to God their feelings of anger and aggression broadly understood and their sexual feelings and desires. In this chapter I want to indicate ways of helping ourselves to become more transparent with these vital and central aspects of ourselves.

I have already alluded a few times to the difficulty of expressing anger to God, especially if the anger is directed at God himself because of life's hurts. One of the strongest blocks to a more personal relationship with God is repressed or suppressed anger and resentment at some of the unfairness life deals us. We might resent being the second-born in the family where it seems the oldest gets all the attention and where we always seem to be second best. We may resent the loss of a parent in childhood through death or divorce. We may have grown up as a member of a harassed minority. We may have a physical deformity or blemishes that have made us the objects of stigmatization by others. Even if our heads tell us that God is not to blame for these lacks, still they are life's hurts, and the anger and resentment we feel may also be aimed at the Author of life. At the least, we may at some level feel that God, the all-powerful, could have spared us or protected us if he really loved us.

After the honeymoon of the foundational experience of God's love has spent itself, these feelings of anger and resentment may surface in us. Along with the fear of expressing anger at God we now may also be inhibited by feeling ungrateful to this God who seems to love us so much. We will find, however, that unexpressed anger will become a massive wall between us and God.

Just think what happens in any close relationship when you are hurt and angered by someone you love, and you are inhibited from expressing the hurt and anger. The relationship gradually becomes polite and bland, more and more distant. You may hope that the other notices the coolness and realizes what he or she has done. Where before you shared many thoughts and feelings and experiences, now your interactions are conventional and boring. You talk more about the weather and other external things. For instance, you may notice that gossip about others replaces personal sharing. What is going on? Because your friend or spouse is so important to you, you are reluctant to express your hurt and anger. You do not want to lose him or her, and you fear that you will if you express your resentment. You may even blame yourself for feeling this way. At root what is going on is a lack of trust that the relationship can stand the open eruption of angry, resentful feelings between the two of you. Until the relationship is tested, that lack of trust will continue to erode the relationship. The relationship may, as a result, die of boredom rather than anything else.

The same kind of thing can happen in our relationship with God when unexpressed anger and resentment lie like a wall between us and God. Boredom in prayer is often a sign of such suppression. Whatever else one may say of God, he is not boring, nor are we when we are our true selves and trust in the strength of God's love for us. An extended example may help.

Anne is in her early thirties and is engaged to be married in six months. She was born and raised Catholic, but had been on the fringes of religion until a few years ago when she experienced a conversion to God. A friend had asked her to go on a weekend retreat and during it she was suddenly confronted with the question, "What am I doing here?" "Here" meant "on earth." She was bowled over by the realization that God had made her out of love and placed her on earth out of love. After that weekend she began to develop a conscious relationship with God. A year later she began to see a woman for spiritual direction. Since her engagement she has noticed that she is quite distracted when she tries to pray and that God seems distant. She even wondered whether God disapproved of her plans to marry, but felt that was an odd idea.

Once when she and her fiancé were talking about the wedding ceremony, she felt a great sadness that her own father would not walk down the aisle with her. He had died suddenly of spinal meningitis when she was eight. Three years later her mother remarried; Anne had never liked her stepfather and did not now relish the thought of his walking down the aisle with her. That night, before sleeping, she started to cry; she still missed her father after all these years. As it turned out, her prayer became distracted and dull right around this time. Her sessions with her spiritual director began to get difficult. She had nothing to say, except that God seemed distant. The director tried to help her to talk about her feelings about this distance. Anne thought that she was just distracted by the plans for the wedding. But the director sensed a note of anger in her voice, which Anne quickly denied.

Another time the director asked Anne to recall the last time when she had felt the presence of God. Anne remembered it and then remembered the night when she and her fiancé discussed the ceremony. When she mentioned her father, tears came to her eyes and she said, "I wish he hadn't died." Gradually Anne came to admit that she was angry about her father's death and her mother's remarriage, but she could only voice the anger indirectly. Then one day she stopped to pray at the church where she was to be married. As she tried to praise God, images of the wedding began to flood her mind. With a flash of rage she saw herself walking down the aisle alone, showing everyone what God had done to her when he took her father. Then the anger boiled over and she told God off in no uncertain terms. She must have stayed in the church about forty-five minutes; she was not sure how long. When she left, she felt strangely relieved. As she reflected on it, she realized that God had heard her out patiently and, it seemed, with great compassion. Now as she walked home, it felt as though he were right beside her. He knew how painful it had been for her and sympathized with her. Periodically over the next few weeks Anne's anger would flare anew, but each time God seemed to be present to her and to absorb her feelings with compassion. The wall had broken down. Prayer was no longer boring.

Experiences such as this are repeated over and over again in people's lives. Some undesirable feeling arises in them that sets up a barrier between themselves and God. They may not recognize right away the connection between the feeling and the barrier, as Anne did not. But if they keep trying to reestablish the relationship with the Lord, eventually the feeling will out, and the relationship continues to develop. A spiritual director can be very helpful at these times. We shall return to this point later. Once again I want to underscore that one clean breast of the feelings did not rid Anne of the anger. It recurred periodically over the next few weeks and had to be expressed again and again. Is this not how things go in any relationship when there is deep hurt that has been unexpressed for a long time? We should expect such recurrences also in our relationship with the Lord.

Besides anger and resentment at God directly, other aggressive feelings can get in the way of our transparency before God. We can become enraged or jealous or unforgiving toward other people and feel unable or unwilling to speak of these feelings with God. Since such feelings have a tendency to be all-absorbing unless we distract ourselves, we will find them arising during prayer too. In fact, we may be unable to concentrate on anything else. If we are afraid or ashamed to admit to God how we feel, we may be unable to pray at all. We may also not want to admit how we feel because we are afraid that God will demand that we change. Again we need to try to be patient with ourselves and to recognize our desire to be "good" before the Lord as a block to prayer. We can ask his help to be more honest about how we actually feel. It will take time, for example, to admit that we would like to smash to a pulp someone we should love. After all, we have been taught from childhood that such feelings are bad. To express such feelings is to court punishment, especially from God, we have been told. The trouble is that we cannot will away such strong feelings; as a result we may be deterred from prayer for a long time. What can we do?

A short reflection may help us to begin the unblocking process. I feel murderously angry at my older brother because of something he did. The incident brings back a host of related feelings that go back to childhood. In the heat of the rage I will, of course, forget all the good times that also occurred, the favors he did for me and even the times he stood by me when I was in trouble. If I bottle up my rage, I may never recall the good things, and our relationship becomes cold and distant. But I do not want to kill him or blow up at him the way I feel now. Where can I turn? I maintain that the safest place to turn is the relationship with the Lord. Over and over again I have seen the following pattern occur as people develop a trusting relationship with the Lord. The undesirable emotion arises and, because it cannot be expressed, creates a block in prayer. "I can't tell God I want to murder my brother." Since the feelings are so strong, however, I cannot do anything else in prayer either. For instance, I try to ask God to help me forgive him, but I really do not mean it. So then I ask God to help me be honest about myself. Slowly I tell him what has happened, and as I do, the anger builds up so that finally I am shouting at God how much I hate my brother. After a while I become aware of what I am doing and realize that the Lord is still there, patiently hearing me out. He is not judging me or badgering me to forgive. He is just listening attentively. I begin to recall some of the times my brother helped me, and I even smile at my rage. But the rage returns and I repeat the same pattern of prayer. After a while I ask the Lord for help to know what to do. It may take time and some face-to-face confrontation with my brother to heal the breach, but the dialogue with the Lord has been healing and helpful to move me toward that end.

We say that the Lord is a healing presence; how can we put what we say into practice? When we feel these strong, aggressive, hateful emotions, we might be helped by contemplating the scene in Mark 5:1–20. Here a man with a demon rages in front of Jesus. The evangelist describes how chains cannot hold him and how night and day he cries out. It is a frightening picture. Yet Jesus does not cower or run away. He calmly approaches the man, and at his word the man is healed. We may not see ourselves as possessed, but some of our aggressive feelings can seem as out of control. Yet Jesus just listens and heals. The safest place to go with our aggression is to the Lord who can help us to channel it toward useful ends. Repressed aggression can leave us like time bombs ready to explode.

Sexuality is another aspect of ourselves that can block the development of our relationship with the Lord. If it can be very difficult to tell God that I despise my brother, how much more difficult it often is to tell him that I lust after someone? Many of us have been brought up to be prudish about sexual matters. Even ordinary things like pregnancy might not be alluded to in "polite company." Some might have very little experience of talking about sexuality except in furtive conversations with the "boys" or the "girls." Moreover, in an older tradition of spirituality sexuality was nothing but a temptation in prayer, and we were told that any sexual thoughts, images or desires should be quickly banished from the mind. Even when people have developed rather healthy ways of discussing sexuality, it may still seem strange to think of talking to the Lord about the topic.

Yet we are sexual beings, and sexuality can be a problematic area in our lives. A poor self-image can revolve around the size of one's penis or of one's breasts. If I am to talk to God about any feelings about myself, I may have nothing to say if I cannot speak of these sexual characteristics. The powerful feeling that focuses all my attention may not be anger at my brother but a strong attraction to his wife. I may feel sexual arousal toward her while I am praying. If I cannot speak of this openly with the Lord, the only recourse may be to quit praying. It has happened that a person's developing relationship with the Lord hit a brick wall when the next step required admitting to the Lord that he or she was homosexual in orientation.

Once again we need to be patient with ourselves. Not everything need be said at once. I can ask the Lord for help to overcome my fears of revealing sexual aspects of myself. I can then gradually approach the hardest part for me to reveal. Around sexual issues a lot of other emotions crowd in: shame, joy, anger, desire, fear, etc. As I reveal myself sexually, I may find myself touching at new levels issues of self-image, especially of myself in relationship to the Lord. There may be a great need for healing since our sexual identity is so bound up with childhood events that are often beyond our recall. Some people have found unearthed long-buried masochistic and sadistic images that have conditioned their image of themselves as bad. In the process of revealing themselves to the Lord they have found that God could handle and heal their most frightening feelings. The light shines in the darkness, and the darkness cannot overcome it.

It happens, and perhaps oftener than we would expect, that the encounter with God or Jesus itself arouses sexual feelings. When it happens, it can be frightening to a person. But perhaps it is only to be expected. When God and Jesus are experienced by us, they are experienced by us who are sexual beings. So sometimes our reaction can be sexual or at least erotic. Here again the best policy is transparency. I let the Lord know what his presence seems to be doing to me and how I feel about that.

Strong emotions, if they are seen by us as somehow not fit for "polite company," can get in the way of a growing relationship with the Lord. The solution is to try to move the Lord out of the category of "polite company" and into that of intimate friend to whom one can tell everything, or at least try to tell everything.

8

How To Begin;
Where To Pray

Many people wonder how they should begin to pray and where they should pray. If we take seriously the notion that prayer is conscious relationship, then we may find some relatively simple solutions.

In his remarkable little book, *The Simplicity of Prayer,* H. A. Williams tells his audience to start: "Here I am again" and then go on to tell the Lord what is going on with you. And this gives us the best clue as to how to begin. If you call up your best friend, there is a reason. You either want to ask how the friend is, or to tell the friend how you are, or both, or just to spend some time together. You do not need elaborate rituals or ceremonies. "Hi, it's Joe. How are you?" We can do something similar with the Lord. We can begin by asking him to make his presence felt, something like dialing the phone. Often prayer books advise a moment of recollection, of recalling the presence of God. I believe that they mean what I just indicated, sort of "dialing the Lord's number" with the hope that he will make his presence known. The moment of recollection will also give us a chance to become aware of why we are calling, that is, what it is we want and how we are feeling at this time.

When we are connected, as it were, we can do pretty much what Williams suggests. "Here I am again, Lord. I want to spend a few minutes (seconds, a half hour, whatever) with you. I'm feeling pretty good (bad, happy, confused, etc.) today. What I'd like to do is to get to know you a bit better (or to get some comfort or healing from you)." Depending on what we want and how much time we have we take different tacks. If I want to get to know Jesus better, then I might take a text of the gospels, read it and let it start my imagination going as we described the process earlier. If I want comfort, I might just start to pour out my heart to the Lord or I might ask him to speak to my heart as he spoke to the Israelites in their troubles, e.g., "Comfort, comfort, my people" (Is 40:1). The point is that we need neither elaborate ceremonies nor large amounts of time in order to enter a relationship with someone we love. All we need is the desire to be in touch and then make some move that allows the touch.

While it is true that we can relate deeply with someone we love in a very short time, at the same time we have to recognize that quality relationships need quality time to develop. If you and I have only five minutes together, you may not want to bring up a topic that seriously affects our relationship because we cannot really deal with it. So too with the Lord. If we want to develop the relationship to deeper levels, we may have to set aside longer times or at least develop the capacity to invite his presence with us while we work or do other necessary chores. A very helpful resource for busy people is *Noisy Contemplation* by William R. Callahan, a book in tabloid form which has down-to-earth suggestions for prayer. Let me suggest one way that the latter might work.

I am in a quandary as to how to proceed with my parish priest. He seems to block every move we parishioners want to make to bring more life to the parish. I have been on the parish council for two years and have been getting more and more frustrated. The last straw came last night and I am really in a stew and thinking about resigning as have all the other effective members. More and more of the parishioners have either given up going to church or go to church elsewhere. I am angry at God, too, for allowing such authoritarian types to get in the way of people's desire to worship him well. The trouble is that I have a busy day ahead of me. The house is a bedlam in the morning as everyone tries to get ready for school and work. I talked to my wife about the situation before we went to sleep, but I feel that I have a bone to pick with God and also that I don't know what is the best thing to do for the parish and for myself. While my wife is showering, I take a few moments to let the Lord know my grievances and ask him to be with me during the day as we thrash it out. In the car on the way to work I concentrate on the traffic, but I do remember my frustrations a number of times, and I get the sense that the Lord is listening. For some reason I don't feel as irritated anymore, but now I want to figure out what to do. As I go from the parking lot to work, I tell the Lord that I'm not sure what tack to take, whether to resign or to stay on to keep trying to change the situation. Again I ask him to stay with me during the day and to give me light. Periodically during the day my mind returns to the issue of the parish. At one point I think of what we have accomplished during the past two years; it is not a total loss. At another time I get a clear sense that the Lord wants me to know that no matter what I decide he will be with me, and I feel very free. At lunch time I have a few minutes free on my way back, and I drop into church to continue the dialogue.

I do not need to prolong this story. I hope that we can see the possibilities in the approach. It requires a relatively well developed relationship with the Lord. This kind of prayer takes seriously the presence of God at any moment and comes as a result of developing a habit of regular contact with him. I might add that this kind of prayer is greatly enhanced by a short review at the end of the day, a chance to look back over the day to see how God was present to me and what my experiences of him might be telling me about the direction of my life. John Carmody makes some excellent concrete suggestions for such an end of the day review in *Re-Examining Conscience*. In the example, I might, by such a review, get a clearer idea of what to do regarding the parish council by noting the gamut of emotions and thoughts I had during the day when I became aware of the Lord's presence. For instance, when did I experience more peace and hope?

The question of where to pray may already have received at least a partial answer. Close relationships do not stand on ceremony, nor do they require special places. There used to be an old joke in which a clever Jesuit, instead of asking his confessor whether he could smoke while praying, asked, "Can I pray while smoking?" The joke was intended to play up the casuistry of Jesuits. It is a pretty stale joke, but I can use it as an entrée to underline the fact that one can pray while doing anything if doing it does not make it impossible to be conscious of the God who is present to every action we do. Thus, one can pray sitting, lying down, kneeling, walking. One can pray while eating, drinking, taking a bath, smoking. One can pray in bed, in a church, in the kitchen, out of doors. As long as I can be or become conscious of God, I can pray anywhere.

The better question for any of us to ask is: Where is the best place for me to pray given the actual circumstances of my life? Note all of that question. It does not say: where is the best place in all the world for me? We are often held back from relating to God (as we can be from relating to others) by waiting for the "perfect wave" as it were. "I would pray if only I had a place to myself," or "if the church were not so far away." If we want to relate to God, then we have to make do with the best reality we can get, just as two poor students on a date may have to make do with a pizza parlor rather than a candlelit restaurant. But "making do" does not mean that we do not try for the best we can in our circumstances.

Close relationships often are nurtured by special places. Husbands and wives may treasure time before sleep not just for lovemaking but also for verbal communing. Friends may have a special walk or park bench they like. There are natural rituals that develop in any close relationship. So too with the Lord. Certain places and certain actions become special because of religious experiences that occurred there. So we return to them over and over again. The magic does not always work, nor do we expect it to, but we remember the magic moments and are grateful.

Here are some of the special places people have found. Particular churches captivate people either because of the atmosphere created by the architecture or because of the personal and generational history associated with the place. Some people find the woods a special place, others the seashore. Some people have sensed the immense presence of God while looking at the stars, others while contemplating a single flower. One man I know imagines the Lord present as a companion while he is driving. One woman likes to have a cup of coffee with the Lord at the kitchen table after the morning hubbub has subsided and before she goes about her daily work. One man has a favorite chair in his office where he sits for a while each day alone with the Lord.

Once I heard someone say that the Chinese search for the jade ring through which they can speak to God and God to them. All of us are looking for our jade ring, a place and perhaps a method for meeting God. Let us encourage one another in the search, but let us also recognize that God, the ever greater Mystery, will always have new surprises, new jade rings, in store for us. We may find him in the most surprising places.

9

Answers to Prayer

In the gospel of John there are a number of spectacular answers to prayer. One of the most spectacular is the raising of Lazarus from the dead, Jesus' response to an unspoken request of Martha and Mary. Has it ever occurred to you though that there may have been any number of bereaved sisters who made explicit requests to God which were not answered by a resurrection of the dead brother? And, truth to tell, Lazarus had ultimately to die and to stay dead; so all the petitions in the world do not stave off death permanently. In this chapter I want to discuss petitionary prayer and God's response to it because these have a strong bearing on the development of our relationship with God.

We have already alluded to the issue of petitionary prayer in the first chapter. God does not need information; so our petitions are not to let him know that, for example, Aunt Jane is dying. Something else is involved. It is a question of trusting that God wants to know my feelings about Aunt Jane's illness and about Aunt Jane herself. I may not want my favorite aunt to die. If I think about it at all, I will also not want Aunt Jane to suffer and drag on a miserable life just for my sake. What do I want for Aunt Jane? As I talk to God about her and about my feelings for her, I may come to realize that I want for Aunt Jane what I would want for myself under the same circumstances, to die peacefully if she must die now, to know deep within herself that God loves her and is with her, to know that I care deeply about her.

Let us note what has happened. Once I begin to experience prayer as personal relationship, I begin to petition God differently. Where before I might have just made a petition and hoped for the best, now I pour out my concern, my desire not to lose Aunt Jane, and then I wait for God's response. In the quiet I may get a sense that God is listening and cares for Aunt Jane and me. The thought may come, "But I don't want her to suffer," and again I sense God's compassionate agreement. I realize that he did not and perhaps could not stop Jesus from dying, and I feel compassion for him. It dawns on me then that I want for Aunt Jane what Jesus must have had and what I want for myself, namely, a deep sense of being held in the mystery of love even while facing the pain of illness and the terror of death.

So what is petitionary prayer? It begins with my concerns and presents them to God, but it also takes into account the fact of a real relationship with God. I bring myself with all my relationships and concerns before God, and in the dialogue with him come to know him better and know better what his attitudes toward my concerns and my world are. I am slowly weaned from expecting magical solutions and begin to prefer the adult food I receive in the form of a better grasp of his relation to us and to our world. As people develop in this way, they are surprised at God's seeming attitudes. Recently two different people told me that they experienced God as compassionate and sad at their plight. The sadness surprised them, but also consoled them. Nor did they feel that God was any less God for this sort of helpless sadness.

We live in a world where "bad things happen to good people" (to use Rabbi Kushner's famous book title). We do not like to see the world in this way because the "bad things" may, out of the blue, happen to us. Psychologists and sociologists point out that most people operate with an unconscious "just world hypothesis" as a result. Like

Job's friends we assume that there must be a good reason for the "bad things" that happen. So the victim must have sinned or made a mistake that could have been avoided. In other words, we engage in an activity called "blaming the victim." In this way the "just world hypothesis" is preserved, and we can breathe more easily about our own chances. We whistle past the graveyard, as it were. But those who engage God directly, as well as those who, like Job, find themselves suffering bad things without any proportion to their sins or mistakes, have the "just world hypothesis" ripped from them. They see that Jesus, the sinless one, suffered horribly, and no bolts of lightning killed his tormentors or saved him. As they develop their relationship with God, they may find themselves raging at him for the suffering they themselves undergo and even more for the suffering others experience. Somehow or other they discover a God beyond what we conceive as justice, a God they can hope in and live for. No more than the author of the Book of Job can they explain it; but for sure it is not the answer proposed by the "just world hypothesis." As a result their petitionary prayer loses all trappings of magical hoping; it has more the flavor of communing together with God about one's friends, one's enemies, one's suffering brothers and sisters throughout the world. And it leads one to doing what one can to try to make the world an actually more just place.

People who have developed such a relationship with God experience the deep mystery of creation and co-creation. God loves into existence not only the stars that so bedazzle us in the night sky but also the volcano that erupts suddenly and engulfs a whole city killing twenty thousand people, and he loves those people into existence. God not only loves into existence Jesus and Mary, Francis of Assisi, Teresa of Avila, and the lovely people who have loved us in our lives, but also Herod and Herodias, Genghis Khan, Lucrezia Borgia, Hitler and the torturers of political prisoners of our day. People who meet this God at a deep level sense a bottomless compassion and pain at the heart of the world, yet a vibrant hope for life. They become more compassionate and passionate themselves. Perhaps they can understand that it was not bravado that kept the martyrs joyful in their sufferings and dyings. Perhaps, too, they can understand how the poorest of the poor still are capable of tremendous acts of generosity toward their fellow sufferers, just as they can understand the great cruelty they are also capable of.

I started this chapter by noting that I would speak of petitionary prayer and God's responses. To be truthful, I am rather surprised at the turn the chapter took once I spoke of praying for Aunt Jane. As I look back now, I realize that I have been describing the process and the results of treating prayer as conscious relationship. Over and over I have seen the process move in the direction indicated. Until I sat down to write the chapter I had not clearly realized that the development of petitionary prayer is as clearly in the direction of mutual revelation as is the more contemplative prayer whose direct purpose is to ask God or Jesus to reveal himself. As I reveal my concerns to him, so too, if I listen, God will reveal his concerns, his attitudes to me.

Doctrine and Prayer

It is rather unfortunate that Christian ministers, and especially Roman Catholics, have seemed more interested in getting doctrinal words used rightly than in helping people to experience the God they believed in. Karl Rahner, one of the great Catholic theologians of this century, once remarked that seminary education did not fit a man to preach a homily on Trinity Sunday in a large city church. And he was right. The catechism and seminary theology taught us all the right words so that we could speak in an orthodox way about the Trinity. But in our lived religious experience we probably have been and perhaps still are functionally modalists, again a point made by Rahner. What does this mean? That in our relationship with God the words Father, Son, and Holy Spirit are interchangeable names for the same reality, Mystery itself, God. If we have experienced some differentiation in the one Mystery, we may not have reflected on it enough to recognize in at least some dim fashion that we were experiencing the differentiation of the Trinity. It may be a help to our relationship with God to spend some time reflecting on the experience of God and its relationship to doctrine.

If we are functional unitarians as we begin to develop more consciously our relationship with God, so be it. It is the reality we bring to the relationship. An analogy may help. I have heard that Martha Smith is a very intuitive, honest person whose very presence evokes a sense of awe and mystery. People have told me that they felt that she could see into their hearts and that they were better persons for having met her. I am impressed by what I have heard, but I have not yet had the experience of meeting Martha. So I am not exactly sure what they mean. Then I meet Martha and experience the power of her presence, and now I know what the others meant. Analogies limp, and badly, when the comparison attempts to make sense of an experience of God. But some insight may be gained from the analogy. If I have not developed my relationship with God to the point where the names Father, Son, and Holy Spirit refer to different experiences of the one God, I may be in a similar position with regard to God that I was in with regard to Martha prior to meeting her. I have heard the Trinity spoken of and I do not doubt it. I just have not had any experiences of God that would give me a clue as to what the doctrine means; and truthfully it does not impinge much on my life. This is my reality, as I begin to develop a more conscious relationship with God. God will have to teach me how to relate differentially, if that is necessary to our developing relationship.

It may even be that prior experience makes it rather difficult to approach God as Trinity. I have met people whose experience of their own fathers had been rather dreadful. They could not imagine God as Father and so latched on to Jesus as God and prayed to him. As they became more and more comfortable with Jesus, they could then take more seriously the undoubted fact that he had a relationship to someone he called "Abba" (Dad or dear Father), and they could ask Jesus to help them to relate to his Father. Each of us need only be ourselves as we approach God and let God lead us from that starting point.

In fact, we usually only find out what our real starting point is by actually relating. The woman who got depressed every time she read the bible only discovered her actual mistrust and fear of God by trying to relate to him through the bible, his word. So too, we only find out that we are functional unitarians by relating to God and noting what really happens when we do. Also we only find out our real attitudes toward the Father, Jesus, or the Spirit by relating. As any relationship develops, not only do we learn more about and become more aware of the other person, but we also learn more about ourselves. For example, in the beginning of a friendship we may only be aware of our attraction to the other. Only later do we become aware of feeling irritated at the other or jealous of the other's accomplishments. The more we pay attention to a relationship, the more fine-tuned we become in differentiating our own reactions. We become more discerning, in other words. The very same thing happens as we grow in our conscious relationship with God.

Perhaps I can give some hints to help that discrimination of the Trinity in experience. I do this, not to say what ought to be, but to encourage readers to pay attention to their own experience to catch, as it were, the "rumor of angels" (the felicitious phrase Peter Berger uses as the title of one of his books).

First let us ask some questions that may help us to recognize that we have had a God-experience or "Abba" experience. Have you ever felt overwhelmed with gladness and a sense of the wonder of life, or awed by the immensity of the universe and at the same time felt strangely safe? Perhaps something like this stirred in you when you looked at a baby, especially your own first baby. Perhaps you felt it when you looked at the stars one clear night and realized how small you were, yet felt at the same time safe and saved. Have you ever felt unaccountably loved and desired by "you knew not what," as Sebastian Moore puts it in the book cited earlier, *Let This Mind Be in You?* Have you ever felt that you were on holy ground, in a place where almost spontaneously you felt like saying, "Holy, holy, holy" and yet felt really safe? Here are a few descriptions of such experiences, part of a whole collection of religious experiences gathered through ads by the Religious Experience Research Unit at Oxford University in England.

I heard nothing, yet it was as if I were *surrounded by golden light* and as if I only had to reach out my hand to touch God himself who was so surrounding me with his compassion.

One night I suddenly had an experience as if I was buoyed up by waves of utterly sustaining power and love. The only words that came near to describing it were 'underneath are the everlasting arms', though this sounds like a picture, and my experience was not a picture but a feeling, and there were the arms. This I am sure has affected my life as it has made me know the love and sustaining power of God. *It came from outside and unasked.*

Suddenly I felt a great joyousness sweeping over me. I use the word 'sweeping' because this feeling seemed to do just that. I actually felt it as coming from my left and sweeping round and through me, completely engulfing me. I do not know how to describe it. It was not like a wind. But suddenly it was there, and I felt it move around and through me. Great joy was in it. Exaltation might be a better word. (All quotes from Alister Hardy, *The Spiritual Nature of Man: A Study of Contemporary Religious Experience.*)

What is being described and hinted at here is an experience that has at least these elements: a sense of awe and mystery and a sense that one is safe with that mystery. The nearest analogy we have for such an experience is the experience of being held safely, snugly, and lovingly in a mother's or father's arms. Could this be one instance of the "Abba" experience, Mystery itself as "Dear Father" or "Dear Mother"?

Let us now turn to another set of experiences that may have occurred to us or may occur as we get to know Jesus better. Have you ever experienced Jesus as a Jewish boy or man of his era with all the particularity and limits of being such a Jesus? He really has to learn language and how to be continent as a baby boy. He eats and sleeps and sweats. He laughs and gets angry. He works as a carpenter. In other words, he is experienced as a real human being. And yet there is a difference. We feel awe as we experience this man. Perhaps the experience comes as we contemplate one of the scenes of healing or when in imagination we sense his eyes boring into our hearts. Perhaps we sense in Jesus a union with God that attracts us deeply and awes us. Perhaps we are jarred by the peremptoriness of his "Leave the dead to bury their own dead; but as for you, go and proclaim the kingdom of God" (Lk 9:60). Or we may just be awed by the love in his eyes as he dies on the cross "for me." Such experiences led the early Christians gradually to the realization that Jesus is Mystery itself, yet not "Abba." Perhaps we are indeed Trinitarians.

How do we experience the Holy Spirit? Have you ever felt really depressed or terrified, yet found within yourself the strength to go on without knowing where the strength came from? Have you ever met someone who seemed to care profligately for you and for others and wondered where that love came from? Have you ever met really poor or suffering people and seen a light in their eyes that just did not seem to square with their situation? Have you ever experienced real care and love between people who should by all sociological and political accounts be at one another's throats—for example, a poor black and a poor white or a Jew and an Arab? Have you ever experienced hope, a fierce, clear-eyed hope even when you were most aware that the world could be blown to smithereens at any moment? Have you ever felt the power of the forces of hatred, greed, prejudice and violence in human hearts and wondered how they are held in check? Perhaps in any or all of these experiences we experience the light that the darkness cannot overcome, the Spirit or Life Breath of God that has been poured out into our hearts and the hearts of all men and women.

By paying attention to the religious dimension of our

experience, therefore, doctrines that were just notional to us become real. God himself teaches us and with an "aha" of insight we come to a dim but real knowledge of the truths of faith. Just as reflection on the lived experience of our relationship with God can make us real Trinitarians, so too we can come to a more experiential grasp of other truths. For example, we say that Jesus is our Savior, but we may have only a notional idea of what this means until we actually experience what it means to be a loved and forgiven sinner, until we actually experience the death of Jesus as "for me" with all my selfishness, willful blindness and sin. In another fine book, *True Resurrection,* H. A. Williams does for the experience of resurrection what I have been hinting at with regard to these other doctrines. A resurrection that is merely past (i.e., it happened to Jesus) or future (i.e., it will happen to us), he maintains, is of little interest to us and has little impact on us. So he points to experiences we have that are already resurrection experiences, signs that we are already sharing the new life of Jesus. Once again we see that prayer as conscious relationship involves mutual revelation. God really does reveal himself to us.

11

The Effects of Prayer

Americans are used to looking for results. Our prag-
matism finds it difficult to enjoy something for its own
sake. So the question of the results or effects of prayer is
bound to arise. Some people also wonder whether the re-
surgence of interest in prayer is a cop-out, a way of run-
ning away from the problems of our world. In this chapter
I want to address these issues on the basis of experience.

If prayer is just conscious relationship, then the first
response to the question of results is to say that the question is irrelevant. Do we have to justify spending time with
anyone we love by pointing to its beneficial effects in other
areas of our lives? We engage in relationships because we
are attracted to other persons, not because the relationships will make us better people. In fact, someone who de-
cided to become a "friend" of another person in order to
improve his personality or gain more social graces would
be using another person. Why, then, do we need to see results in order to justify prayer?

People engage in prayer as conscious relationship because they want to know and love God better. At least that
becomes the main motive of relatively mature people. Of
course, we may want God's help in difficult crises. We may
want to be healed of a disease, for example. But at the
deepest level our desire is for a relationship. What surprises people who let God come close is that God, too,

wants a relationship. God is not first and foremost interested in results, but just loves us. One of the fears we have is that God will make demands on us if we allow him to get close. So we want to keep him at arm's length, if not continent's length, from us. Over and over people find that God is love, as the First Letter of John insists. And love is not utilitarian, does not have an ulterior motive. Love desires the good of the beloved, desires intimacy with the beloved. So people discover that God's love is unconditional, does not carry a price tag, and that is surprising and surprisingly difficult to believe.

If the question of results is irrelevant, does this mean that God has no standards, no values, no hopes for those he loves? Does relating to God consciously have no effect on people? Again I direct your attention to what happens in any close relationship. If I love you, for example, it is because I find you attractive. I admire your values, your attitudes, your behavior. The more I get to know you, the more I want to be like you in the qualities I admire. Notice that I want this; it is not because you demand it of me but because I like what I see. So too, as we come to know and love God or Jesus, we want to be like them, not because they demand such conformity as a price of their love, but because we admire them and because we feel more whole and happy the more like them we are.

Thus, the longer people remain in conscious relationship with Jesus, the more like him they become. They are changed for the better. The pattern I have seen recur runs something like this. People need the primordial experience of God as love which I mentioned in Chapter 8. They need to experience at a deep level that God is really on their side. In this initial period of conscious relationship they experience the desire that Jesus heal them and forgive them. As Jesus becomes more and more real to them, they also experience strong approach-avoidance reactions to him. They are strongly attracted by his healing, forgiving love, but they also become deeply afraid that he will find them wanting. There is a sense of waiting for the other shoe to drop, as it were. "Yes, he has loved me up to now, but will he still love me when he realizes that I am _____ (fill in the blank) or that I have done _____ (fill in the blank)?" It often takes a long time for this process to come to a relatively sure resolution. But finally most people who are faithful to the process of developing the relationship come to the deep conviction that Jesus loves them, warts and all, sins and sinful tendencies and all, so much that even killing him would not turn his love aside.

With this conviction comes a shift of focus in the relationship. Where before they wanted Jesus to be where they were, now they want to be where he is. Now they focus more on Jesus himself. They want to know him more and love him more and become like him. They want to be his companion, his friend, his follower. They desire to love as he loves, to forgive as he forgives. In other words, in the traditional language, they desire to become other Christs. So they contemplate Jesus in the gospels and ask to become like him. And gradually they are changed. But it is almost by osmosis, not by grim acts of the will, by grace and gift, not by the strength of their own characters.

People who have come to know and love Jesus in this way do make a difference in the world. They are better spouses, better parents, more honest workers, more truthful and faithful friends. They see the world more honestly and recognize inhumanity and injustice more easily. They are more compassionate, but they are also more passionate to see justice done. They may not be comfortable to be around just as Jesus was not always comfortable to be around. Huub Oosterhuis in one of his prayers calls Jesus "difficult friend." Those who become like Jesus may also be difficult friends in the sense that anyone who speaks the truth may make us uncomfortable.

Gerard Manley Hopkins expressed it this way:

I say more: the just man justices;
Keeps grace: that keep all his goings graces;
Acts in God's eye what in God's eye he is—

Christ—for Christ plays in ten thousand places,
Lovely in limbs, and lovely in eyes not his
To the Father through the features of men's faces.

But it must be remembered that only Jesus is the actual incarnation of God. Even the greatest of saints falls far short of being like him. So ordinary mortals like us who follow Jesus must always reckon with our weakness and our sinfulness. People who have come close to Jesus know in their bones that Jesus knows them through and through and knows that they will always be fallible human beings. But he still loves them and still believes in them and still wants them as his close friends.

Yes, prayer does have an effect on the person who prays. But that effect is not the primary motive for praying. It is a by-product. The primary motive for prayer is love, first the love of God for us and then the arousal of our love for God.

Spiritual Direction

Recently I was asked to respond to the following question by the editor of *Praying*. He has graciously given me permission to reprint my response here.

> I am a lay person and for several years have had the recurring desire to find someone to counsel me in my spiritual life and prayer. I guess I am looking for a spiritual director, although I don't really know what a spiritual director does and thus I am embarrassed to ask anyone. What is spiritual direction and what can one expect from a spiritual director?

Here is my reply. Some of it will be repetitious of what we have already discussed in the book, but perhaps it will serve as a summary of the key points.

Many Christians are asking the same question you ask. In the past twenty years we have witnessed a remarkable rise of interest in prayer and spiritual direction in people of all walks of life. It has been somewhat of an embarrassment to the churches that so few of their professional ministers have been able to respond to the desire of so many for help with their prayer. Perhaps because of the embarrassment, perhaps because God himself has been calling people to respond to the need, centers and programs for training spiritual directors have sprung up across the United States and in other countries, and they can hardly keep up with the demand for such training. As a result more and more of God's people are finding competent help when they ask: "Teach me to pray."

You ask what spiritual direction is. It is a form of pastoral counseling which focuses on a person's relationship with God, on a person's prayer life, in other words. If prayer is defined as conscious relationship with God, then you will talk with a spiritual director about what happens when you are conscious of God. It is as simple and as profound as that. For several years you have had a recurring desire to find someone to counsel you in your spiritual life and prayer. At this point you might ask yourself: "Do I mean that I want someone who will help me to develop my conscious relationship with God?" If your answer is yes, then you are looking for the kind of direction I mean.

This definition of spiritual direction opens the way to describing what you might expect from a spiritual director. He or she would be interested in your actual experience of God, not your speculations about God. So the director would want you to talk about your experience and would patiently help you to do this. We almost have to invent a language to talk about our actual experience of God because we are so unused to speaking about it. The director will ask you questions like these: "What happens when you pray?" "What is God like for you?" "What do you want or desire from God when you pray?" At first such questions may puzzle or even scare you, but gradually, if the director is patient and really interested in your experience, you will find yourself able to articulate more and more of what you experience in prayer.

It's not as though beginning spiritual direction is the beginning of your relationship with God. You already have such a relationship, and it is rather well developed and conscious if you have the recurring desire to seek help with prayer. The spiritual director wants to help you to become more aware of the relationship that already is and more articulate about your experience so that you will know how solid the bedrock of your prayer life is. You will then be helped to pay more attention to the Lord's communications to you and your own reactions to him and to life.

Relationships develop when the two persons involved pay attention to one another and reveal themselves to one another. Your director would help you to decide how you best meet the Lord in the circumstances of your life. The Lord is available at all times and in all places, we believe, but we are not always conscious of his presence. Each of us who wants to develop our relationship with the Lord has to look at how and where we can let him make his presence felt. For some it might be lying in bed just before going to sleep at night or rising in the morning, for some on the bus or train going to work, for some luxuriating in the bathtub, for some walking in the woods, for some stopping at a chapel or church, for some reading the bible. Indeed, any one person might find all these activities (and others) at one time or another conducive to becoming conscious of God.

Often enough we think of prayer as "saying prayers." But prayer can just be silent weeping while conscious of God's presence or listening to the birds or to the wind in the trees or to music. God makes his presence, his desires, his hopes known under these circumstances. So the director will encourage you to ask for what you want, e.g., "I want to feel deeply that God loves me, warts and moles and all," and then to do something that will allow you to be quiet long enough to let God respond. And your director will help you to pay closer and closer attention to your experience by a patient and persistent interest in it. As a result you will grow in reverence for your own experience as the privileged place to meet God.

As you can see, the kind of spiritual direction I describe is not esoteric or even very difficult. It is just a matter of two fellow Christians talking about the experience of God one of them has. Spiritual direction of this kind ought to be much more available in our churches. But, truth to tell, it has not been so available. Even in religious houses and seminaries spiritual direction until recently did not consist of listening to the religious experiences of those directed. Rather the spiritual director was often the confessor for a very large number and, at best, gave good advice when people had problems. I recall one director years ago who began every session with me with the question: "Any problems?" He seemed a bit crestfallen when I usually answered "No." During the time I met with him, we never discussed my actual prayer experience. Small wonder that few priests and religious know how to help another with prayer when they got so little help themselves.

Throughout the church's history there have always been men and women who really listened to the prayer experience of those who sought their help. One thinks of the desert monks, of Teresa of Avila, of the holy woman to whom Ignatius of Loyola refers in his autobiography, of Ignatius himself, of Francis de Sales, and many others. But such listeners have always been in short supply. In our age more and more men and women are trying to learn the difficult, yet simple art of inviting conversations about religious experience. I hope that you will be able to find one of them.

How does one go about it? Ask around. "Are there any spiritual directors in the area?" "Do you know anyone who helps people with their prayer?" If you do find a possibility, ask for an appointment so that the two of you can look one another over and talk about what you want. Even if you begin direction with someone, make an agreement to review together how things are going after about five to seven sessions. The main criterion for you will be whether you are being helped to develop your relationship with the Lord.

13

Conclusion

If you have gotten this far, it is clear that you have a strong interest in prayer. I hope that you will trust that interest and see it as a response to a God who yearns for intimacy with you and who hopes that you will want to develop your relationship with him. Recently it struck me that perhaps the deepest reason why God was so pleased with Jesus was that Jesus let God come as close as any human being could. In other words, to the maximum possible for any human being Jesus let God be intimate with him, let God love him as much as God wanted to and could. This insight gave new meaning to the baptism scene where the Father is heard to say: "Thou art my beloved Son; with thee I am well pleased" (Mk 1:11).

Over and over again people have described to me how delighted God seemed to be when they let him love them, let him get close. What they described was not a utilitarian love by God, that is, a love that is bestowed so that some other good might be accomplished. God does not seem to love Mary Smith, for example, so that she can in some way do good work for the church; he just loves Mary and in loving her makes her to be lovely. If Mary consciously accepts that love, she will be a different person, to be sure, and she will be a more salutary presence in her world. But that change in Mary is a by-product, as it were, not the reason why God loves her and wants her intimacy. Because I heard many such experiences, I had the insight into God's delight in Jesus. Interestingly, the gospels put these words in God's mouth at the beginning of Jesus' public ministry, that is, before he has "done anything," as it were. Perhaps God's delight in Jesus is just because Jesus let him be who he wants to be for each of us, "Abba," "dear Father, dear Mother."

So your interest in prayer must delight God. I hope that you will give him even more delight by allowing the relationship to develop and deepen. Prayer, after all, is just conscious relationship with God, and like any conscious relationship this one too grows through mutual revelation or developing transparency. In the process of getting to know God better, I trust that you, too, will come to realize at deeper and deeper levels that God is a lot better than he's made out to be.

Annotated Bibliography

Readers may find the following books helpful.

Barry, William A. and Connolly, William J., *The Practice of Spiritual Direction.* San Francisco: Harper & Row (Seabury), 1982. Describes the kind of spiritual direction that helped convince me of the usefulness of the model of relationship for prayer.

Bergan, Jacqueline and Schwan, S. Marie, *Take and Receive: A Guide to Prayer.* Winona, MN: St. Mary's Press, 1985–86. Four of the projected five volumes (*Love; Forgiveness; Birth; Surrender*) have appeared so far. In an attractive format each volume begins with a brief description of various forms of prayer and then offers material for daily prayer based on the Spiritual Exercises of Ignatius. For those who like a structured approach offering a variety of options for each day these books can be quite helpful.

Callahan, William R., *Noisy Contemplation.* Hyattsville, MD: The Quixote Center, P. O. Box 5206, 1983. A book in tabloid form that gives helpful hints about how to pray in the midst of a busy and noisy life.

Carmody, John T., *Holistic Spirituality.* Mahwah, NJ: Paulist, 1983. Treats the major areas of life, e.g., work, recreation, politics, as they are integrated into a spirituality whose center is love. Well-written, practical, helpful, and demanding.

Carmody, John T., *Re-Examining Conscience*. New York: Seabury, 1982. A modern approach to the traditional practice of the examination of conscience. Like the previous work well-written, practical, helpful and demanding.

DeMello, Anthony, *Sadhana: A Way to God*. St. Louis: The Institute of Jesuit Sources, 1978. A book of prayer exercises by an Indian Jesuit who integrates Eastern and Western prayer forms. Many have found these exercises very helpful for prayer.

Dyckman, Catherine Marie and Carroll, L. Patrick, *Inviting the Mystic, Supporting the Prophet: An Introduction to Spiritual Direction*. Mahwah, NJ: Paulist, 1981. A good, short introduction to the nature of spiritual direction.

Finn, Virginia Sullivan, *Pilgrim in the Parish: A Spirituality for Lay Ministers*. Mahwah, NJ: Paulist, 1986. A book written by a lay minister, a wife and mother, whose purpose is to help lay ministers move to the heart of all ministries, the mystery we call God, and thus to integrate prayer and ministry.

Moore, Sebastian, *Let This Mind Be in You: The Quest for Identity Through Oedipus to Christ*. San Francisco: Harper & Row (Seabury), 1985. A dense but brilliant work by one of the most original spiritual theologians writing today.

Pennington, M. Basil, *Centering Prayer: Renewing an Ancient Christian Prayer Form*. Garden City, NY: Doubleday, 1980. After a short historical introduction showing its roots in the Christian tradition of imageless prayer, Pennington describes the method of Centering Prayer in a gentle, practical, heartfelt manner.

Praying: A Spirituality for Everyday Living. P. O. Box 410335, Kansas City, MO 64141. A tabloid edited by Art Winter and appearing about every six weeks containing practical, helpful articles and features on prayer.

Williams, H. A., *The Simplicity of Prayer: A Discussion of the Methods and Results of Christian Prayer.* Philadelphia: Fortress Press, 1977. A wonderful little book (which may, unfortunately, be out of print) containing three talks on prayer given at an Anglican parish in England.